Unspoken Expressions From Marie

By. Harmoni Marie

Unspoken Expressions From Marie.

Contents

About the Author
Harmoni Marie

Unspoken Expressions From Marie is a powerful collection of poetry that gives voice to the thoughts and emotions often left unsaid.

Through raw honesty and creative expression, Harmoni Marie explores love, identity, growth, healing, and resilience. Each poem captures a moment, a feeling, or a lesson, inviting readers into a journey of self discovery and transformation.

This collection reflects the balance between softness and strength, vulnerability and confidence, brokenness and becoming. It speaks to anyone who has ever struggled to express how they truly feel, reminding them that their emotions are valid and their voice matters.

Written with authenticity and depth, this book is more than poetry. It is a reflection of real experiences, real growth, and real truth. If you have ever felt unseen, unheard, or uncertain in your journey, these pages will remind you that you are not alone.

SECTION

I

MIX OF EMOTIONS

WHAT CAN I SAY TO YOU?

I told you
feelings just lie.
I tried to get you out my mind,
But that's just wasting my time,
'cause you still pop up in disguise.

But I still recognize your eyes,
And I still recognize your lies
yeah… I think I'm hypnotized.

It's like I miss you,
but I'm so through with that.
It's like I love you,
but don't want to attach.

Feel like I need you,
But I cannot relapse.

Trying not to overthink it,
trying not to overspeak it,
trying to find the words

to let you know
that I really mean it.

But we too damn connected.
You're so cold, and I'm anemic.
Don't want to dream it or think of you,
You just lie, can't tell the truth.

But I still want you to be my boo
nah… my dude.

More like my man,
my helping hand.
You started off as a friend,

Now I want you
till the end.

The worries that overtake me (Written in 2023)

Worrying about the day, worrying about the night,
Wondering if I'll die or have to stay in the fight.
My worries overtake me, my mind is always racing,
The days are always fading.

I didn't ask for this world, it was given to me.
Some nights I ask God,
If He gave me a new life, what would it be?

Would it be hard like this one,
Or easy like the privileged kids
Who act unable to open a bottle lid?

When they get around us, they try to act hard,
But don't got these Black scars.
Even Black people try to act hard
'Cause they don't want to show their pain,

But sometimes you might look at their face
And see the rain

Pouring down into their veins,
Only to know
There's no happiness in this life.

Asking God for help,
But then not even thinking there's Christ.

See, I know this feeling
Asking God,
Is there really a cure called healing?

I don't know.

I just write my feelings as if they were notes,
But to answer your question…

I don't know.

Don't know what God has for me,
Don't know if people feel sympathy or envy for me,
Don't know who my real enemy is

Other than me.

HIS BLUE EYES

Your gaze is my ocean view
The Love we share is fairly new. I know this to be true
because my only thoughts are of you
Your kindness is unmatched, your beautiful soul is intact. I
didn't want to attach, but your pursuit became facts.
Your blue eyes hold stories only my heart can read,
A quiet promise of everything I could ever need.
In them I see peace, a life soft and bright,
Like stars shining boldly in the night.

When you look at me, the world fades away,
And every doubt inside me quickly loses its say.
Your presence feels like home I never knew I missed,
A feeling so pure, I'm surprised it exists.

So I follow your gaze like waves to the sea,
Because somehow your blue eyes always find me.

The Letter I Never Sent

I'm writing this letter because there are things I need to say,
Words that sat inside my heart but never found their way.
I'm not the type to speak my feelings out loud and clear,
But writing feels much safer than pretending they're not here.

I'm on a journey now, trying to grow and uplift my soul,
Learning how to express the parts of me I can't control.
So I'm putting pen to paper, letting honesty begin,
Because silence kept too long can weigh heavily from within.

You said you wanted something real, a serious place to start,
So naturally, my expectations opened up my heart.
But honesty is all I ever truly asked from you,
No confusion about intentions that I thought were true.

I will never chase a man who chooses not to stay,
I know my worth too clearly to give my power away.
It's easy for me to have attention if I choose,
So thinking I would chase you is a thought I'd refuse.

Because I cared, I offered love and effort from my side,
But when it wasn't returned, I slowly stepped aside.
I would never force a place where my heart doesn't belong,
And love should never feel like proving someone wrong.

I only wish things had stayed the way they once began,
Before the silence settled between a woman and a man.
And though the story changed in ways I didn't intend,
I still hope life gets better for you in the end.

SECTION

MY ESCAPE

The City of Light

We found it tucked on the darker side of town,
where streetlights flickered and half stayed down.
A record store with a buzzing sign,
barely glowing, but it pulled me in just right.

Windows dusty, glass cracked thin,
but something about it felt like home within.
Posters peeling off painted walls,
old soul music echoing through the halls.

The door creaked open, a bell rang low,
and time slowed down in that amber glow.
Vinyl stacked high, floor to ceiling,
every corner held a different feeling.

We laughed too loud like we owned the night,
young and reckless under dim streetlight.
Leather jackets, denim dreams,
living somewhere in between.

Fingers flipping through records worn,
each one holding a life reborn.
The needle dropped
and something changed,
like my whole body got rearranged.

It hit my chest, ran through my veins,
a rhythm I didn't know I could contain.
Like I was chasing something I couldn't name,
but somehow… I had felt it before the same.

We stepped outside, still caught in the sound,
like the music followed, like it wrapped around.
That feeling rising, pulling me far

like I was already leaving
for somewhere beyond where we are.

laughing with friends under warm amber sky.

Outside, the street was midnight dark,
but far ahead, a city spark.
Disco lights in a distant glow,
music pulsing, calling my soul.

"Let's go," I said, and we took flight,
chasing the rhythm, chasing the night.
A euphoria pulling me closer still,
like I was flying on pure will.

Feet on pavement, heart in the air,
nothing but freedom everywhere.
I ran, I ran, never slowing down,
chasing that city, chasing that sound.

I woke before I reached the light,
but that feeling stayed, it felt so right.
For years I've chased that secret high,
that taste of freedom I can't deny.

I still hear the echo of that distant beat,
still feel the pulse beneath my feet.
A dream that lingers, soft but strong,
a city of lights where I belong.

Until I find it, I'll keep the pace,
chasing that feeling, that sacred place.
Maybe one day I'll reach those stars
and find that beach on Mars, that disco bar.

But until then, I'll dream again,
and run through the dark
where the lights begin.

Party Lights

Lights flashing, bass blasting, bodies moving fast,
Music shaking through the walls like it might never last.
Laughing, dancing, drinks in hand, everybody free,
Yeah, it looks like a movie… but it's more real to me.

Girls in the mirror fixing gloss, fixing lace,
Boys outside acting bold, tryna find their place.
Phones out, flash on, moments getting caught,
Living in the night like this, all we've got.

And I'm right in the middle with a smile on my face,
But the music hit deeper than the beat and the bass.
Every song feels familiar, like it's calling my name,
Like nostalgia running wild through my veins.

It's a feeling I can't explain,
Like memories turning into a beautiful stain,
Something I carry but don't wanna erase,
A soft kind of hurt I still choose to embrace.

The laughter feels louder when I'm trying not to feel,
The lights shine brighter when I'm hiding what's real.

I move with the crowd, let the moment take control,
While the rhythm temporarily quiets my soul.

For a second, I forget all the things on my mind,
All the weight that I carry, all the pain left behind.
In the chaos, I'm calm, in the noise, I'm at peace,
Like the world finally lets all my overthinking cease.

But when the night slows down, and the party gets thin,
When the music fades out, and the silence creeps in,
I feel it all coming back like it never left me
Every thought, every fear, every memory.

And maybe that's why I love it,
Why I run to the sound,
Why do I lose myself in spaces
where I don't have to be found.

It's a high I can't fight,
a drug I won't name,
a temporary escape
from my own pain.

So I dance a little longer,
stay a little too late,
chasing moments that help me
forget what I hate.

Yeah… I know what it is,
and I know it's not right,

But I'll always love the feeling

of losing myself

in the night.

A Beach on Mars

I found a place that no one knows,
Far from the world and all its woes.
A quiet shore, a distant star,
A hidden beach on planet Mars.
No noise, no pain, no heavy air,
No overthinking waiting there.
Just waves that glow in shades of red,
And peaceful thoughts inside my head.
The sky is soft, a different hue,
A mix of pink and cosmic blue.
No past to haunt, no tears to cry,
Just open space and endless sky.
I lay back slow, feel time stand still,
No pressure here, no need to heal.
No broken hearts, no wrong, no right,
Just me alone beneath the light.
And maybe it's not real or true,
But it's the only place I knew
Where I could go and feel at peace,
And let the weight inside me cease.
So when this world feels far too hard,
I close my eyes… I'm back on Mars.

California Dreaming

California dreaming lives inside my mind,
Golden skies and palm trees, something I'll soon find.
Late nights, city lights, stars within my reach,
A life I've always wanted calling out to me.
Sunsets on the highway, windows rolling down,
Music in the background as I leave this town.
Chasing every dream I used to only say,
Now it feels so real, like I'm on my way.
They say it's far away, they say it's just a dream,
But I see it clear, yeah it's closer than it seems.
Walking down those streets like I already belong,
Like I've been there in my heart for so long.
Bright lights, big stages, cameras in my face,
Living out the life I knew was meant for me to chase.
Every no I heard just pushed me to believe,
Everything I want is waiting there for me.
I don't fear the change, I don't fear the fall,
I was never meant to stay here small.
There's a version of me living in L.A.,
And I'm getting closer to her every day.
So I'll keep dreaming, but I'm working too,

Turning every vision into something true.
California calling, I can hear my name
And one day soon,
I won't just dream…
I'll be living in that place.

After the Party

The music stopped,
the lights went low,
Everybody left,
now I'm alone.

Cups on the floor,
heels in my hand,
Mascara running
I didn't plan.

The laughter's gone,
the silence stays,
And now I'm stuck
with how I feel again.

No music to hide it,
no crowd to pretend,
No distraction
to play my friend.

Just me and my thoughts
in the quiet room

And suddenly
everything feels too soon.

Maybe I don’t love the party,
maybe I love the escape

‘Cause when it all ends…

I still feel the same.

SECTION

LOVE & CONFUSION

Miss Me

Miss me with that sadness,
Really miss me with that sad shit.
You turned me into madness,
Now you're wishing that you had this.

Funny how it changed quickly,
You went quiet, I went savage.
Turned my pain into power moves,
Now I walk like I'm the baddest.

I was soft, I was patient,
Gave you time, gave you grace.
You got comfortable with silence,
I got comfortable with space.

Now I'm glowing, now I'm shining,
And it's written on my face.
You fumbled something real,
Now you're watching me replace.

Miss me with your "I miss you,"
Miss me with your "come back."

You had me when I gave love,
You lost me when you lacked.

Now I'm everything you needed,
And everything you lost.
You had access to the greatest,
But you couldn't pay the cost.

So miss me with that sadness,
I don't carry what you broke.
You created something stronger,
Now I stand in what I wrote.

And if you ever think about me,
Just remember what you missed

You turned me into madness
Now you're wishing
that you had this.

Pink Flowers

The sight of pink flowers reminds me of you,
A sign I once asked from God
to know if you were true.

The need of wanting you
felt long overdue,
Like something meant to happen,
like a dream I held onto.

Honestly, I say I'm over it
that's what I do,
But the sight of you still somehow
turns my skies blue.

Those petals so soft,
but fragile the same,
Like the way I held love
and the way you played the game.

I thought you were a blessing,
a prayer come alive,

But not everything from God
is meant for you to keep in your life.

Now pink flowers bloom
and I don't know what to feel,
'Cause something so pretty
once felt so real.

I try not to look,
try to pass them on by,
But memories linger
no matter how hard I try.

So I let them remind me
of what used to be true

That I once saw something beautiful

When I looked at you.

Cycle

Numb to my feelings,
even more numb to yours.
I'm sorry I had to become your villain,
but that's just my new way of healing.
My heart been cold,
I don't even know when it changed,
Somewhere between feeling too much
and feeling nothing… I rearranged.
I don't react the same,
I don't care like before,
Things that used to mean something
don't reach me anymore.
And it's not about love,
so don't get it confused,
It's just how I move now
detached, unamused.
I see it happening too,
I'm not blind to the truth,
Hurt people hurt people…
and now I'm living the proof.
I don't mean to be distant,
but I don't try to be close,

I don't hold onto feelings,
I just let them all go.
It's like something switched off,
and I can't turn it back on,
Like I'm stuck in between
who I was and who's gone.
I don't ask for connection,
I don't care if it stays,
People come, people go
I'm the same either way.
And maybe it's wrong,
maybe I'll feel it one day,
But right now I'm just here…
and this is my phase.
So don't take it personal,
don't question what's real
I'm just caught in a cycle
of not wanting to feel.

I Almost Said It

I almost said it,
but I held it in,
Didn't wanna start something
I couldn't win.

I almost told you
how I really feel,
But some things sound better
than they are real.

So I stayed quiet,
let the moment pass,
Some feelings don't need
a future to last.

And even though
it stayed unspoken

Some silences
still leave you broken.

WHERE DO YOU WANT TO BE

You can try to play it off, act brand new,
But I still got a hold on parts of you.

You can't fake what we used to be,
You can't erase that history.
She might have you, but not completely…
There's still pieces that belong to me.

Tell me does she know your pain?
Does she feel you when it rains?
Or is she loving surface-level things…
While I still echo in your veins?

You don't gotta say it, I can tell it's true,
Late at night you still think of me too.
Tryna fill a space that don't fit right,
But you know exactly what to do.

When it's quiet and you can't sleep,
When her love don't run that deep
You know where I'll be.

I been acting like I moved on fine,
Like you don't ever cross my mind.
But truth is… it hits sometimes,
Like old feelings I can't decline.

I don't mean to still feel this way,
Don't mean to care, don't mean to stay.
But something in me won't let you fade…
Even when I try to walk away.

We both know this ain't brand new,
You play your part, I play mine too.
Act like we don't need each other,
But we circle back like we always do.

And I hate it
But I crave it.

That tension we never could break

I don't mean to love you still,
Don't mean to feel what I feel.
But if I'm being honest…

I probably always will.

All of Me, For You

From the moment I saw you,
something changed in me,
Like a feeling I never thought
I'd ever believe.

I don't fall easy,
I don't lose control,
But you touched something
deep in my soul.

And I can't explain it,
the way you make me feel,
Like everything around me
suddenly turned real.

You got this magic
I don't understand,
But I don't wanna fight it
I just wanna hold your hand.

I'd do anything for you,
no hesitation, no fear,
If you call, I'm coming running,
you just say you here.

I'm not playing games,
I'm laying it all out,
Every feeling, every thought
no holding back now.

Whatever you want from me,
I'm giving it all,
No halfway love,
no fear of the fall.

You got my heart
in a way that's new,
And I don't even mind…
'cause it's safe with you.

You make me feel like
I'm floating above,
Like I finally understand
what it means to love.

Not rushed, not forced,
just natural and right,
Like something meant to happen
in this moment, this time.

And I don't need forever
to know this is true

If I give my heart…
I want it with you.

So take me as I am,
every piece, every part,
I'm not scared to fall
if it's into your heart.

I'm all in, no hesitation,
no need to pretend

If this is love…

Then I'm yours
again and again.

SECTION

IV

EXPRESSIONS

Freestyle (Get It Back)

And oh no baby I ain't scared,
I needa get my mind right, tryna make it out of here.
You think that you see it all, but your vision ain't that clear,
If you knew the things I did,
you probably wouldn't be here—
But oh well.

I'm tryna get my shine back,
Needa get my grind back,
I can't get my time back,
Just wishing I could rewind that.

Late nights in my head, yeah, I'm fighting what I feel,
Trying not to break down, trying hard to keep it real.
Had to learn the hard way, pain taught me the deal,
Now I move a little differently,
now I know what's really real.

I was giving too much love, I was losing who I am,
Now I'm picking up the pieces, putting focus back on me.

Had to step away from everything that
couldn't let me breathe,
Now I'm walking in my purpose,
now I'm finally feeling free.

I don't dwell on what I lost, I just focus on what's next,
Every lesson turned to blessings, and every L became a flex.
I was down, but never out, now I'm rising with respect,
And the pressure made me better;
now I'm nothing like the rest.

So I'm getting my shine back,
Yeah, I'm getting my grind back,
Can't go back in my time,
So I'm moving where my mind at.

And oh no baby I ain't scared,
I've made it through the storm, I'm still standing right here.
Now my vision is getting clearer
And the girl I used to be?

She's just floating in the air.

Speaking Into Existence

I speak it before I see it,
I claim it before it's mine,
I trust what God has written
It is already aligned.

I am financially successful,
I am happier than ever,
I am living my best life,
And it only gets better.

I am in the best shape,
mind, body, and soul,
I am becoming everything
I once prayed to hold.

I am dating my soulmate,
a love that's real and true,
the kind that feels like peace
and still excites me too.

I am fabulous, focused,
I am flourishing in grace,
I stay in my own lane,
can't nobody take my place.

I am unbothered, glowing,
clear skin, beautiful light,
I love myself fully,
I'm stepping into my right.

I am healthy, I am wealthy,
I am confident, magnetic,
everything about me
feels powerful, energetic.

I am strong and protected,
I am wanted, I am seen,
I am everything I dreamed of
and everything in between.

I am worthy, I am free,
I am loved, I am whole,
I radiate confidence and grace
from my spirit to my soul.

Every year will be my year,
I can feel it, I just know,
God is doing something greater
Watch how everything unfolds.

There is favor over my life,
There is glory in my name,
There is restoration coming,
nothing will be the same.

Past years were a lesson,
But He carried me through,
and I trust what's ahead of me
It is bigger than I knew.

So I speak it into existence,
every dream, every vision I see

Because everything I prayed for

is already

Becoming me.

"Summer Like This"

That feeling you don't rush.

Sun shining, skin glowing in the heat,
Windows down while the music on repeat.
No stress on my mind, just peace in the air,
Ain't thinking 'bout nothing I'm just there.

Days feel longer, nights feel light,
Everything slow but it still feel right.
Laughing with my people, no worries in sight,
Just living the moment like every day's mine.

Riding through the city, breeze in my hair,
Good vibes only, yeah we don't care.
Everybody outside, looking their best,
Summer got a way of making life feel blessed.

It's something about it…
you can't explain,
The way it bring back memories
you didn't know you saved.

Cookouts, music, dancing all night,
Talking 'bout old days under streetlight skies.
Smell of the grill, laughter in the air,
Moments so simple but you wish you could stay there.

Kids outside playing, running around,
Music from somewhere, that familiar sound.
Family close, everybody smiling,
Time slow down, just for a while and

You realize…
this what life's about,
Not the stress, not the noise, not the doubt.

Just being present, just feeling free,
Just you, your people, and good energy.

And I don't need anything extra or new,
These moments right here already feel like truth.

So I sit back…
and let it all unwind

'Cause nothing feels better
than a summer like this.

SECTION

V

BREAKING POINT

Waiting Room

I'm sitting in a waiting room,
trying to breathe,
trying to think,
on the way to the bathroom
But really… trying not to fall apart.

My mom is in surgery,
And I don't know how to hold
all these feelings at once.

I'm stressed.
I'm scared.
I'm sad, angry… heartbroken.

Because at the same time,
You left me.

Like it was nothing.

I didn't think it would hurt like this,
didn't think it would feel this heavy.

It's not fair
None of it feels fair.

I don't even know
How am I going to get through this?

But I keep saying
I'm trusting God.

Even while I've been crying
day and night,
trying to understand
How something I felt so deeply
could disappear so easily for you.

Now I'm left here
questioning my worth,
wiping tears
That doesn't seem to stop.

They say it's God's protection
But right now
It just feels like pain.

Still…

somewhere inside me
There's a small piece of hope.

A quiet kind of peace
telling me
There's something greater,
someone better,
Someone meant for me.

And even though I loved you…

Maybe it just wasn't meant
To be.

So I sit here,
holding onto faith
with shaking hands,

hoping one day
this pain
Just makes sense.

3AM

It's always 3AM
when my thoughts get loud,
When I'm alone
but feel surrounded by a crowd.

Every "what if"
starts playing again,
Every memory
feels closer than then.

I stare at the ceiling,
lost in my head,
Thinking 'bout things
I wish I never said.

But morning comes
and I act like I'm fine

Like I don't lose myself
every night at this time.

God, is it Over?

It's over…
at least that's how it feels.
Like I crossed too many lines,
like I can't undo what's real.
If I could go back, I would
fix what I knew wasn't good.
I'm here now…
and I don't recognize who I became.
And if I'm honest
I've been mad at You.
Trying to stay strong
but feeling lost too.
If You save sinners…
then what about me?
I'm trying, but failing repeatedly.
So can we go back
not to who I was before,
but to something real…
something more?
And maybe…
it's not over.
Maybe grace still covers me,

even when I don't feel worthy.
So I close my eyes
If You still see me…
then I know
it's not over.
it's not over.

What Time Really Means

Lights off...
just me and everything I don't know.
I heard about God,
heard He sees it all,
but sometimes it feels like
He ain't picking up my calls.
I be so caught up in time
or what I think time means,
chasing moments, chasing dreams,
chasing everything in between.
They wear gold on they wrist,
but don't even realize what they miss
we track time...
but don't value it.
I wish I had time,
then waste what I got,
like I'm guaranteed more
when I'm really not.
And that's scary.
Time don't rewind,
don't pause, don't wait

every second that passes
is sealing your fate.
So now I move different,
more aware, more still
Not just chasing success…
but purpose,

and something real

SECTION VI

The Healing

Seen in Christ

Hair done, nails done, outfit on check,
Look in the mirror like, "yeah… I'm set."
Picture look perfect, angles on ten,
But why do I still not feel it within?

Smiling outside, but inside it's loud,
Trying to feel worthy in front of a crowd.
Posting for validation, chasing a view,
Hoping somebody might see something true.

'Cause if they don't like me… then who am I?
If the likes go down… does my worth decline?
If I'm not the image they want me to be,
Do I still matter… or disappear quietly?

I tried to define me by what I could wear,
By how I looked and how people would stare.
By attention, affection, who chose to stay,
By who walked in… and who walked away.

But that kind of identity never feels right,
It fades in the dark, it shifts with the light.

It builds you up quick just to tear you apart,
Leaves you empty… right back at the start.

I'm not what I wear, I'm not what I own,
Not the highlights I post or the life that I show.
I'm not what they say, I'm not what they see,
There's something much deeper inside of me.

And I had to learn
I don't have to perform to be loved,
Don't have to compete to be enough.
Don't need the world just to tell me I shine,
When God already said, "you're mine."

See, I was searching in places that couldn't fulfill,
Trying to fill spaces only He could heal.
Looking for worth in attention and praise,
But losing myself in so many ways.

Now I stand different, I move with peace,
Not chasing approval, I finally breathe.
'Cause my value don't come from a trend or a name,
And it don't decrease when they don't give me fame.

I know who I am, yeah I'm grounded in truth,
Not based on my past, not based on my youth.
Not based on mistakes or what people assume,
But based on the love that pulled me through.

So when I look now, it's not just my face,
It's purpose, it's grace, it's more than a place.
It's knowing no matter what life may bring

My identity…
is not in this world

It's in Him.

HEALING ISN'T PRETTY

Healing isn't pretty,
it don't look cute,
It's crying in silence,
it's feeling mute.

It's losing yourself
before you grow,
It's sitting with pain
you don't want to know.

It's letting go slowly,
not all at once,
It's learning to walk
when you used to run.

So don't rush healing,
just take it slow

Even broken things
still learn to glow.

The truth about the rain
Rain doesn't ask
if you're ready to feel,
It just falls heavy
and makes it real.

Just like emotions
you try to ignore,
They build up slowly
then hit you more.

You can run from it,
hide if you want,
But feelings don't leave
they just confront.

So I stand in the rain,
let it fall through

'Cause sometimes the storm
is what makes you.

Freedom in the Sky

Window seat, headphones on,
watching the world as it moves along.
City lights blur into lines,
like memories I left behind.

I press my head against the glass,
thinking 'bout how fast things pass.
All the people, all the places,
all the names, all the faces.

Some I loved, some I lost,
some came with a heavy cost.
Some felt real, some felt fake,
some were lessons I had to take.

The plane takes off, I close my eyes,
leave behind what didn't feel right.

And somewhere between
where I was and where I'll be

I feel like I'm finally
Becoming me.

SECTION

VII

More Of Marie.

The Harmoni Marie Edition

Yours Truly

I always knew…
I was the best.

Guess that was a lucky guess…
No, I'll say this with my chest
There was nothing lucky about it.

I passed every test
And now?

I'm happy to announce
I'm next
Yeah… next up.

People ask me my motto

I just look at them and say

I never gave a fuck.

It was never luck.

I'm just blessed.
Really…
I am the best.

Not to boast

I just do the most.
While they watch, I'm ahead of the rest.

So let's toast.

No really…

Let's toast.

To the growth.
To the confidence.
To becoming everything they doubted.

A Toast to me…

The one…
and only…

Harmoni Marie.

Dancing Queen, Young & Sweet

Dancing queen, young and sweet,
Living life on reckless feet.
Laughing loud, no fear, no shame,
Every night a different game.
Music loud, the lights are bright,
Living fast inside the night.
Phones out, capturing the scene,
Trying to hold what life has been.
Late night drives with songs on blast,
Talking 'bout how long this lasts.
Dreaming big, no time to sleep,
Promises we swore to keep.
We didn't know how fast it'd go,
How quickly we would have to grow.
Those little moments, free and wild,
Felt like forever for a while.
Now I look back and I can see,
That girl still lives inside of me.
Young and sweet, still chasing dreams,
Still dancing through life's in-betweens.

So here’s to nights we can’t repeat,
To being young, and wild, and free
Forever a dancing queen in me.

More than

More than a pretty face,
more than a skinny waist,
more than a race
that I win first place.

More than the image
you see from afar,
more than the label
of who you think I are.

More than the looks,
the likes, and attention,
more than the moments
you choose to mention.

I'm more than the body,
more than the frame,
more than the beauty
attached to my name.

More than the smile
I show in the light,
more than the version
you see in the night.

I got thoughts in my head,
I got dreams in my soul,
I got things I've been through
that you'll never be told.

More than the wins
that you choose to praise,
more than the highlights
of my best days.

I'm strength, I'm growth,
I'm lessons, I'm pain,
I'm everything I lost
and built back again.

So don't box me in
or reduce what you see
I'm more than a moment,

I'm fully me.

THE ME I HAVEN'T MET

There's a version of me
I haven't met yet,
She's everything
I can't be just yet.

She walks with peace,
she moves with grace,
You can see the light
just on her face.

She don't overthink,
she don't second guess,
She knows her worth
she accepts nothing less.

She lives in places
I've only dreamed,
Living the life
I've always seen.

And every day
I get a little closer to her

With every lesson,
every scar, every blur.

One day I'll look up
and finally see

I didn't chase her...

She became me.

Mrs. Hollywood

They call me Miss Hollywood, like it's just a name,
Like I woke up one day and stepped into the fame.
Like the lights found me easy, like the shine came free,
Like this life that I want just fell onto me.
They see the gloss, the outfits, the way that I move,
The confidence I carry, like I got something to prove.
They think it's all pretty, all bright, all good,
That's why they label me "Miss Hollywood."
But they don't know the nights we ain't have a place,
Or the tears I had to hide just to keep up my face.
They don't know the struggle, the weight that I stood,
They just see the shine and call it Hollywood.
They don't know about moving, about breaking apart,
About watching a family fall piece by heart.
They don't know depression or the thoughts in my head,
Or the nights I laid awake wishing I wasn't there instead.
They don't know what it took just to keep going on,
To still wake up smiling when everything felt wrong.
To carry my dreams when life never would,
And still believe I'd make it to Hollywood.
So call me Miss Hollywood, say it out loud,
But know it was built from pain I made proud.

Every tear turned vision, every hurt turned plan,
I became who I am ‘cause I knew that I can.
I’m not just the image, the lights, or the mood,
I’m strength, I’m survival, misunderstood.
And one day when I make it like I said I would
You’ll see why they called me
Mrs. Hollywood.

That Girl

Sometimes it feels like they all want a piece,
Want my time, my attention, my glow, my peace.
But I'm only one girl, I can't split in two,
Still they stare like I'm something they're trying to pursue.

Got the look, got the vibe, got the light in my face,
Walk in a room and I shift the whole space.
They don't know my name but they know my vibe,
Like they seen me before in a dream in their mind.

I'm that girl
The one they can't quite define,
That girl
Always dancing through minds.
That girl
Style so crazy, can't find,
Another one like me, Nah, I'm one of a kind.

When I move, feel the floor rearrange,
Like the world gotta shift when I step in my lane.
Eyes locked in, yeah they stuck on me,
Like I'm something they seen but can't fully reach.

It's the way that I walk, it's the way that I shine,
Like confidence dripping in every line.
I don't try, I just am, that's the difference you see,
I don't follow the wave, the wave follows me.

To them I'm a star, I don't gotta pretend,
I don't play any role, I don't bend just to blend.
I'm just me no filter, no mask, no fear,
And somehow that's what brings everybody near.

I'm that girl
The one they dream late at night,
That girl
Never dimming her light.
That girl
Everything feels so right,
And they swear they could see me if they
close their eyes tight.

SECTION

A Dream With Granddad

In the dream, it was just me,
walking into a room as bright as morning.
Your voice rose first,
familiar, strong, filling every corner.
I turned, and there you were:
healthy, glowing, smiling like the man I've always known.
I waited to hug him, to hear him say my name the way he always did.
I asked him to preach to the world, to let everyone witness his wisdom.
He smiled, sat in his chair, and I lay my head on his lap.
Light poured over my face, warm and soft,
and I felt peace fill my body, the kind that stays.

I thought about the ones waiting for you
Grandma Dolly, Aunt Debra, your brother,
And even my Nana, Dianne
all gathered, ready to welcome you home.
And I knew you'd meet them with that same smile,
that same calm faith you carry.
In that moment, it didn't feel like a dream.

It felt like home, like love, like everything he taught us,
and I knew, even when he leaves this world,
The light he gave us will keep shining.

Even as the dream faded,
The warmth stayed.
You told me we won't fail,
that your lessons live on in us.
You'll be wrapped in love,
and we'll carry your light forward,
until we meet again.

My Wonder Woman

My mama is my superhero,
my real-life Wonder Woman,
not the kind in movies
the kind that keeps going
even when life keeps coming.

She made something out of nothing,
turned pain into a plan,
built a life with her bare hands
when no one else could understand.

She's loving, she's caring,
but stronger than they see,
The kind of strength you only learn
when life don't let you be.

She's been through storms
that could break a soul in two,
But somehow she stood tall
and brought me through it too.

She didn't just survive,
she became everything she dreamed,
A woman full of purpose,
more powerful than it seems.

Smart in every way,
wise beyond her years,
Carrying generations of strength
through every silent tear.

She's my best friend,
the one I always run to,
The voice that speaks life into me
when I don't know what to do.

She taught me how to stand,
how to fight, how to believe,
How to trust in God's timing
even when I couldn't see.

She's success in human form,
not just money, not just fame,
But the way she built a life
and still remained the same.

And if I ever become
half the woman she is

Then I know I did something right
just by being her kid.

So this is more than a poem,
this is everything I see

My mama, my hero,

my forever
Wonder Woman to me.

Sharks Don't Swim Backwards (A lesson from Granddad)

Family sitting around you,
Thanksgiving air was heavy with stories,
and I told you about my heartbreak.
How it felt like I'd lost something I couldn't get back.

You smiled and said, "Remember when I used to go fishing?"
I nodded.
And you said, "There's something I learned about sharks.
They always swim forward.
They can't go backwards, because if they do, they'll die."

You let that sink in.
"Think about that," you said.
"There's no need to go backwards.
You just keep moving forward,
for what God has waiting for you."

Now I think about that every time I want to turn around,
Every time I miss what I shouldn't return to.

Sharks don't swim backwards
and neither should I.

So I'll keep moving forward,
even when it's hard,
trusting that what's ahead
is better than what's behind.
And I'll carry your words like a compass,
knowing that forward is the only way to live.

A GOOD DAY, ALL THANKS TO G.O.D

Today was a good day,
I feel peace about everything,
about all the things I prayed for,
and all the things still happening.

I might not be feeling my best,
still learning, still finding my way,
But I can feel it in my spirit
Everything's getting better each day.

Every worry feels lighter,
every doubt slowly fades,
and even in the quiet moments
I see the change God made.

So I thank Him for the progress,
for the strength I didn't see,
for reminding me in His timing
Everything is working for me.

Today was a good day, not perfect, but I'm okay.
And that alone is enough to say…

I'm getting better.
All thanks to God.

www.ingramcontent.com/pod-product-compliance
Lightning Source LLC
La Vergne TN
LVHW010939110826
845149LV00013B/2675

* 9 7 8 0 9 9 9 3 7 9 1 3 4 *